LIVING
THROUGH LOSS

God's Help in Bereavement

DAVID WINTER

Harold Shaw Publishers
Wheaton, Illinois

All Scripture, unless otherwise noted, is from the *New International
Version.*

Grateful acknowledgement is made to the publishers of *The Holy Bible:
New International Version.* Copyright © 1973, 1978, 1984 International
Bible Society. Used by permission of Zondervan Bible Publishers.

ISBN 0–87788–507–9
Cover photo. Luci Shaw

Library of Congress Cataloging-in-Publication Data
Winter, David Brian.
 Living through loss.

 1. Bereavement—Religious aspects—Christianity.
2. Consolation.   I. Title.
BV4905.2.W56 1986   248.8'6   85–26212
ISBN 0–87788–507–9

96 95 94 93 92 91 90 89 88 87 86
10 9 8 7 6 5 4 3 2 1

CONTENTS

INTRODUCTION

It was about three o'clock on an October afternoon. I had spent most of the day in a studio, making a radio program, but as soon as I got back to the office my secretary told me that my wife, Christine, was on the phone. I picked it up, assuming that there was some errand she wanted me to do, or some change of plans for the evening. I was totally unprepared for what she said: "Your mother has died."

I didn't say anything for a moment, and so Christine asked, "Did you hear?" I said, "Yes, but it's a bit of a shock." At that she began to cry, and it was only then that the fact, rather than just the information, really hit home. My mother was dead.

She had died suddenly, at home. Apparently she had gone to the door to answer the milkman's ring, and at that moment dropped dead. She fell in such a way that neither the milkman nor a neighbor who came to help could open the door, so it was some time before anyone could try to treat her. In any case it was useless. She had died instantly of a massive heart attack.

As I drove through the north London suburbs to her home I experienced that strange sense of numbness that others had often described to me. Life was going on as normal all around me. No doubt the late-afternoon traffic was as heavy as usual, and people were unloading trucks, pushing strollers, repairing shopfronts, selling and buying newspapers. But I was not part of it. Cocooned in my car, I went through the motions of driving, but I have no recollection of any details of that journey.

My mother was elderly and had suffered from angina off and on for several years. But she was still active, mentally alert, and very unwilling to be regarded in any way as old, let alone senile. I suppose we must have accepted that one day during the next decade or so she would die, but this sudden death left me in an unexpected state of shock. As I drove, my feelings were numbed, but my mind was at work recalling images and memories and reacting in a variety of ways to those thoughts. The one thing I seemed incapable of accepting was that my mother, who had been an inescapable part of my life for forty years, was now no longer a part of it.

When I got to the house, my older brother was already there with a couple of the neighbors. My mother's dead body was lying on a bed in the front room not a dozen feet from where she had fallen to the floor an hour or two earlier. My sister-in-law made tea for everyone. The rector arrived, followed by the funeral director. The routines of death and bereavement had begun to take over, but I felt like little more than a spectator.

Within two or three hours of death, the body was taken away in a black hearse with a gold cross on the side. We went into the neighbors' house and drank whiskey—not a drink I like, but it helped to bring out as yet unreleased feelings. The neighbor, a man we had known since we were toddlers, began to cry. He told us how he felt he should have done more for our mother, that he could see her lying there, but he couldn't get the door open. My brother and I watched his grief but in a strange way could not share it. He was regretting a human failure, a circumstance which had prevented him from helping an old friend at the moment of her direst need. His grief could be assuaged. The whiskey helped, and so did the repeated assurance that even his immediate help would have made no difference at all. The doctor had assured us that mother died instantly.

The rector prayed with us, and we were grateful for his presence, but at that precise moment the consolations of faith could not infiltrate the numbness of shock. I don't suppose that I wavered from my belief that my mother would share in the resurrection of the dead and life eternal, but it simply wasn't in the forefront of my concern. Later that night I was able to pray; within a day or two faith was my most valuable weapon in facing bereavement. But there is a time and a place for everything, and this was a time for slow and gradual acceptance of the fact of death.

I lost my father many years before my mother's death, when I was a student. A middle-aged man, he died after a terminal illness of several weeks and a lifetime of heart trouble that began when he was gassed as a teen-age soldier in the First World War. He had died in the same house as my mother. His body had lain on the same bed in the same room.

My father's death activated a different kind of bereavement in me. Knowing that he could not possibly recover, we had time during his illness to accept the situation. The pain of loss was just as great; there was this same numbness during his last weeks and in the days preceding the funeral, as though I had been anesthetized and was living in a state of suspended animation, aware at one level of what was going on around me, but not feeling a part of it.

However, the more drawn-out experience of watching someone die is very different from the trauma of sudden death. I don't think one is easier than the other, but the process of realization and acceptance when someone close to you dies is definitely affected by the circumstances—just as the death of a young person creates a different kind of shock from the death of an old person who is full of years and "ready to go."

I begin this book on bereavement with these two experiences most vivid to me because, quite honestly, that seems the best place to start. Bereavement is not an abstract concept, some sociological or psychological phenomenon to be analyzed and examined. It is an intense human experience, and one that sooner or later everybody shares. It has been part of the human lot since the dawn of human history, and no amount of medical knowledge or psychiatric support is going to eliminate it. In one sense we are not fully human until we have been bereaved, for it is the apprehension of our own mortality that makes us what we are and distinguishes us most clearly from the animals, who seem to live oblivious of death and largely untouched by their own or their companions' mortality.

We are not so oblivious. We have, and are deeply affected by, a knowledge of death. No theme is more deeply woven into the poetry and drama and religion of our race, and that is as true of modern man as of his ancient forefathers. Dylan Thomas, in a poem of desperate passion, pleaded with his dying father:

Do not go gentle into that good night,
Rage, rage against the dying of the light!

Indeed, modern man finds death even more difficult to cope with than his predecessors did. Death stubbornly refuses to be mastered. With technology we have subdued and utilized the environment and even the building blocks of matter itself, but mankind remains mortal. He may well rage at it, but the fact is that the light of life *does* die, and what Thomas describes as the "night" does indeed close in on all of us in the end.

Bereavement, the loss of someone we love through death, is a universal human experience. It can have a fearful, and sometimes quite unexpected, impact on those who experience it. While most people eventually weather the problem, some are left permanently embittered, mentally crippled by the event itself or their reaction to it. Sometimes bereavement can distort or destroy relationships among those who are mourning; sometimes, sadly, it can lead to the dissolution of an apparently genuine religious faith, leaving its victim cynical, faithless, and angry.

On the other hand, and more commonly, a person looking retrospectively at a time of bereavement can see how it has strengthened him and helped him grow. Many people have come to a better and healthier understanding of themselves, or of those they love and depend on, through their loss. It is a necessary part of the cycle of human existence, and while it is always sad and sometimes tragic, it need not be a bitter or destructive element in our lives. Accepted and understood, the experience of loss can actually help us to appreciate life more fully. It can build faith and help us to understand ourselves, other people, and God in a fuller and more mature way.

This book is about bereavement, but in fact it is more precisely about our *reaction* to bereavement. It is about how we can live with the loss of a loved one, and how we can help and support others who have to do so. And it is a *Christian* approach to bereavement: showing how faith in God and in Jesus Christ can provide a healthy, positive, and creative response to death, a response which does not ignore the real pain and grief or evade the inevitable sense of deprivation, but looks beyond it in faith and hope.

1

THE SHOCKING EVENT

DEATH COMES IN A THOUSAND FORMS. We all know that it is inevitable, yet it often manages to take us by surprise. About one in every five deaths is sudden. Roughly half, on the other hand, occur in hospitals. The most common cause of death is heart failure, and cancer is the next most common. Every year between 40,000 and 50,000 people in the U.S. die from traffic accidents alone.

Nearly two million people die every year in the U.S. Assuming that each person has four close relatives or friends for whom his death is in a real sense a bereavement, then eight million people go through the experience every year. It is estimated that a psychologically healthy person needs almost two years to recover from the effects of the death of a loved one, so at any given moment there may be about sixteen million people—almost one in fourteen of the American population—who are suffering to some degree from the effects of bereavement. In this sense the mourner is never alone. The experience of loss is shared by all of us eventually, and the actual process is one most adults have gone through.

The first reaction to the death of someone close to us is the numbed shock I have already described in my introduction. If the death is sudden or the circumstances unexpected—a child dying in an accident, perhaps, or an apparently healthy person dying after a sudden heart attack—we may well reject the idea at first. Often the initial words spoken by people when they are told of such a death are, "Oh, no!" The mind refuses to accept such a stark and unwelcome message.

In one sense this is a normal reaction and is the product of the body's own defense mechanisms. The fact is too awful to contemplate, so the mind protects itself with a kind of anesthetic layer. The very shock which the news induces becomes a protection. Everything in the real world assumes an air of unreality which helps us keep the unwelcome truth at a manageable distance.

This explains why very often the closest relatives do not at first seem as upset as other friends and neighbors. Shock has dulled their response. For hours, even days, they may seem relatively unmoved, and people may be tempted to suggest that they are taking it very well. In fact, they are not "taking it" at all. The full truth of the situation has not yet penetrated the defensive wall around their mind. The time for outward grief has not yet arrived.

Sometimes this period of rejection is less passive. The instinctive "Oh, no!" becomes a violent "It can't be!" The shocked mind searches for a scapegoat in a desperate attempt to resist the inevitable. This may lead to hurtful or blasphemous statements: it's all the fault of the doctor, the nurses, the paramedic, the husband or wife, the too-demanding employer. Or it's all God's fault.

If this happens, it is important that friends and professionals involved with the bereaved person do not take offense. Most doctors are familiar with this reaction and disregard it, but friends and relatives may be hurt or outraged by such unfair accusations. This is not the time to argue the matter, however. The reaction must be seen as an irrational defensive gesture. Certainly anything said by a bereaved person in this first stage of shock should not be held against him, or allowed to destroy valuable relationships later on. We may be sure that God does not take offense at such remarks. It may be harder for human beings to overlook them, but it is something we must try to do.

This anger is probably our way of externalizing an inward sense of loss. We have been hurt, and this is a way of ensuring that others are hurt, too. Seen in that light, it may appear vindictive: but in reality it is more defensive than aggressive, and few bereaved people maintain these complaints once the initial shock has worn off.

In the usual pattern of bereavement, very quickly, often within an hour or two of the death, a social process is set in motion which involves the closest relatives of the deceased without destroying the protective cocoon which envelopes them. The funeral director brings a calm but usually reassuring professionalism. The rector, priest, or minister will often call. Neighbors and close friends will visit or offer refreshments or housing for relatives. And, ideally, the family will quickly "move in," with those who are less personally involved taking over the domestic duties and providing a background of normality.

It is important to allow bereaved people this time of numbness. There should be no pressure put upon them either to express grief or to withhold it. Sometimes at this stage they will be anxious to talk about the circumstances of the death, but not about their own reactions to it. The great value of having friends and relatives in the house is that they can provide conversation, refreshments, and an air of normality, without excluding the bereaved person. The strain of keeping up appearances, or even making conversation, is removed from him.

I have mentioned the ideal circumstances. Surveys suggest, I'm glad to say, that the great majority of bereaved people *are* supported by their families, and, to a lesser extent, by their friends and neighbors during the trauma of the first few days after a death. In a survey in the Lichfield Diocese in England, it was found that about 64 percent of the sample of bereaved people were given significant help by their families over this period, and about 20 percent received similar help from friends.

On the other hand, some people have to survive the experience of bereavement under less than ideal circumstances. The same survey shows that the most difficult loss to cope with is the death of a spouse. When a couple is elderly and living far away from the rest of the family, the surviving partner may find the first day or two of bereavement a desperately lonely experience. Often such people no longer have social contacts outside the home, perhaps because of failing health, and consequently they may have few friends nearby. It is hard for neighbors who have barely been on speaking terms to suddenly assume the difficult and sensitive role of supporting a bereaved person. It is in circumstances like these that shock can affect a person so severely that it delays recovery for months or years. Sometimes, sadly, the surviving partner has no will to recover and simply drifts along, dying within a few months.

It is dangerous to underestimate the shock of bereavement. In a particularly moving book, Christopher Leach describes his own reaction to the sudden and tragic death of his eleven-year-old son:

> The time between his death and the result of the post-mortem was like a landscape visited by a slow-moving, fluctuating mist, settling in the hollows of our days, thickening so that many hours were spent blindly— tasks performed automatically because they had to be done—and then the mist would clear abruptly, and the fact would appear again and have to be faced again . . .[1]

As Leach discovered, there is no short-cut through this experience. The "mists" he speaks of are in fact merciful. The facing of the awful fact can be only partial at first. Friends and relatives need to allow the bereaved person to move in and out of these levels of knowledge at his own pace.

There may be a temptation for a Christian to try to bring a more positive element of faith into the situation. I believe there is a time to speak of such things, and a time to be silent. Individual cases are each different, of course, but generally, those who counsel the bereaved—including clergy and ministers—agree that during this period of initial shock it is simply love, companionship, and practical support that is most needed. Later, there will be plenty of time and opportunity for reflection on the wider, Christian aspects of bereavement.

Religious advice, if given insensitively, may actually be harmful. Leach, who has no religious beliefs, was visited by a woman, a stranger, on the morning after his son's funeral:

> She had heard of our sorrow. She was plainly dressed and her face was polished clean, free of make-up. In gloved hands she carried two books, which she said we

must have. They would explain everything. There was no need to mourn. There was a purpose in everything. God had simply called him home early. God needed him. She was almost vehement in her desire to comfort us. Her bright eyes shone with conviction. She *knew*.

I took the books, and thanked her . . . I read the first page, and was not comforted.

Quite apart from the content of her advice, much of which seems to me to be dubiously Christian, the timing of her approach was manifestly wrong. We can expect that we will say the wrong thing sometimes—in fact, it is inevitable, and seldom does any lasting harm. But it is essential to choose the right time, especially when we are dealing with someone who is in a state of shock. To tell a bereaved parent or wife that "God has taken" their loved one is to invite blasphemy. Later, they may well see things in such a light, but at the moment of deprivation, far from being a comfort, the idea is almost a provocation.

To offer Christian care to the bereaved during these first hours and days we should concentrate on three things. First, we should make ourselves available as constantly as possible. Unless he insists on it, the bereaved person should not be left alone in his house or apartment. Simply being there, helping with visitors, answering the phone, making tea or coffee, and ensuring that the ordinary routine of life goes on is a service of infinite value.

Secondly, we should pray: pray *for* the bereaved person and, if he agrees, *with* him as well. Many people in the shock of loss find that they cannot pray. God seems momentarily remote and the coldness that has gripped their emotions makes it hard for them to open themselves to him. Often, however, they will find it helpful to share in the prayers of someone else—not prayers necessarily about the death of their loved one, but ordinary prayers of trust and confidence, and of intercession for others. Joining in the Lord's Prayer or reading a psalm may also be a help. But if the exercise appears to be unduly painful, abandon it. God understands their situation perfectly, and he will not abandon them. They will turn back to him in prayer when the mists begin to clear.

The third service we can render to the bereaved person is to help him talk through the circumstances of the loved one's death and remove any feelings of guilt he may have about it. Time and again during the period of shock, I have heard bereaved men and women remonstrate with themselves: "If only I'd taken his illness more seriously . . . I should have called the doctor sooner . . . I wish I had tried to persuade him to give up work . . . I should never have let her go out on that wet day the previous week." Seldom, if ever, is there any reason for this self-recrimination, but it is part of the process of apportioning blame. Death is an enemy to mankind that we cannot bear to see overpower us.

As we talk over the circumstances of the death with the bereaved person, we can help him realistically work through the causes and reassure himself that he has no reason to feel self-recrimination or guilt. It may be that the bereaved person will want to go over the story repeatedly. Let him. Far from being morbid, this can be very therapeutic. Let every ghost of guilt be thoroughly exposed and resolved. This may also include anger at the medical services for some seeming delay or failure. Here, though, we should beware of agreeing with such accusations in the hope that it will somehow mollify the bereaved at this stage. If there is, by any chance, some ground for complaint, it can be taken up after the funeral. Usually, however, once the initial shock is over, the anger evaporates and often turns to appreciation for the care offered by medical personnel.

For the bereaved person, these first hours and days are going to be difficult. There is little advice that can be given—certainly *not* "Keep a stiff upper lip," or "Take hold of yourself." Nature has its own way of cushioning the blow: the numbness that I have described often pervades all that is happening. The bereaved person may find himself surprised that he is not more upset and he may even feel guilty on that account. In fact, the deeper the wound, the greater the degree of numbness. This will eventually pass, and the pain and grief may well become more severe, but in these first hours the greatest need is to survive, to lean unashamedly on those around us, and to trust—unconsciously, if need be—in the love of God.

Finally, we need to realize that the bereaved person may not be the only one suffering from shock. Very often the relatives of the bereaved person are also suffering, but they see the symptoms (a drawn face, cold hands, loss of appetite, withdrawal, sluggish movements, silence) only in others. Shock does not affect everyone in the same way, of course. Some will be talkative, even irritatingly so. Others will have few external symptoms, but experience the numbness beneath a veneer of normality. We should not judge; nor should we assume that the degree of grief can be measured by the evidence of external symptoms.

Practical Considerations
Almost from the moment of death there are practical things to be done. According to the Lichfield study, nearly 70 percent of all bereaved people become involved in making these practical arrangements, either alone or with a relative. This can be a good thing, for it provides a distraction and

a duty at a time when to sit and do nothing would only underline the sense of loss.

If the patient died at home, and the doctor must be contacted. He will complete the death certificate, unless the death was so sudden that he hadn't been treating the patient immediately before the decease. In the latter case a postmortem will have to be performed, but the doctor and the funeral director will make those arrangements. Often in the case of a sudden death the doctor will inform the police. Usually this is no more than a formality, but obviously the police must be involved if there has been an accident or there is some question about the cause of death.

Usually the second call should be to the funeral home. It may be that the next of kin has no preference in the matter, or no knowledge of local services. Their names will be in the yellow pages, and it is advisable to choose one who belongs to a recognized professional organization (National Funeral Directors' Association).

Funeral directors are available day and night, and will usually remove the body within a matter of hours to their own premises. They are accustomed to calling at homes of the bereaved, and generally have a kind of detached seriousness and professionalism which makes their dealings with the family as painless as possible. Certainly they should quietly and efficiently take over, relieving the family of much of the anxiety about practical arrangements.

However, one has to say that a funeral is an expensive affair. It is practical for a relative or friend who is *not* so intimately involved to discuss the question of cost with the funeral director. People undergoing the shock of bereavement are inclined to agree to anything, or even to regard any discussion of price as somehow insulting to the memory of their loved one. There is no point in taking on enormous expenses unnecessarily, and a simple conversation with the funeral home will usually establish what sort of costs are involved. That is no more than ordinary prudence.

After the funeral home has been contacted, those who are Christians, or who know that the person who has died had church connections, should contact their priest or minister. Again, he will not mind being approached at any hour as he may wish to call at the house and minister to the family. In any case, if a church service is desired, along with the usual committal at the cemetery or crematorium, it is advisable to let your minister know as early as possible, and also to inform the funeral director of your wishes. Otherwise it will often be assumed that no church service is desired.

Within a few days a death certificate will be prepared. Normally the funeral director will make arrangements for this. It is usually worth paying an additional fee to obtain several copies of the death certificate. These will be needed for claiming any social security insurance, death grants, pensions, or allowances. Having several copies will save a great deal of time and trouble.

Notifying employer, friends, and distant relatives by phone call or letter is another time-consuming task. A notice in a local or national newspaper can be a means of letting a wider circle of people know of the death.

It is already obvious that a death in the family creates a number of unusual tasks. Doing them may seem distasteful at the time, but in fact the occupation they create, and the effort they require, can be blessings in disguise. Quite simply, they leave less time for sitting and thinking!

On the whole, we can be grateful for these practical and social tasks and for the defense mechanisms of the human constitution. The initial stage of bereavement will pass, probably quite quickly. The real grieving, and the real test of character and faith, lies ahead. Like the crew of the ship carrying St. Paul to Rome, caught in a violent and unexpected storm, we too may be well advised to "drop four anchors from the stern and pray for daylight."

2

NOT THE END

IT MAY SEEM A FOOLISH QUESTION to ask, "What is death?" After all, it is common enough. From early childhood we are familiar with the inevitability of death—flowers die, our favorite pets die, and sometimes, neighbors or relatives die. Unless a child loses an adult to whom he is close, there is no need to explain to him what "death" means. It is the end of life.

Yet there *is* a need to answer the question, because the way we understand death—at any rate, the death of human beings—will determine how we react to it. If it is the end of everything, the extinction of existence much like the extinguishing of a candle's flame, then death is the ultimate and irreversible defeat. Its foreboding shadow lies across the path of life like an ominous cloud. Into every relationship and every hope or ambition enters the doubt and fear of inevitable death. If the moment before death is the last moment of existence, then this life is all we have, and the best thing we can do about those we love who have died is to forget them.

On the other hand, if we believe that death is the means by which we enter a new life, and that this new life is one in which relationships with loved ones on earth have a continuing and enhanced existence, then we mourn our separation from them but look ahead to a time when we shall see them again. The ordinary pleasures and joys of life do not have that tinge of desperation—they become a foretaste of the real thing that lies ahead. Death may bring pain, tears, suffering, and sadness, but it is not an enemy. Its arrival is not a defeat. For us the words of St. Paul are a cry not of defiance, but of assurance: "Death, where is your sting? Grave, where is your victory?"

Physically, death is, of course, the end of the body. Laid low by disease or age, or broken by accident, its vital functions cease and an irreversible process of disintegration begins. Christians and unbelievers agree about this: there is no future for the flesh and blood which make up our earthly bodies. To quote St. Paul again, "Flesh and blood cannot inherit the kingdom of heaven." Our bodies are designed for life on earth. They are of no use to us beyond it—certainly not in heaven, which is a spiritual environment.

So our bodies perish. That should not worry us too much, especially after we have begun to experience the effects of aging. We can't shake off infection so readily. Our memory isn't so good. Unfamiliar aches and pains afflict us. Our bodies tire more easily; we can't move quickly or run for the bus like we used to. The process is gradual, but it is also irreversible, and many elderly people look forward to death, not morbidly, but as a release from this process of physical decline. Eventually, however much we reject the idea, the physical bodies we have lived in since birth must be laid aside. Indeed, the idea of an immortal body, living on through decade after decade of old age, strikes most of us as grotesque.

But to say that the body dies is not to say that the person ceases to exist. I will return to this idea later, and have written more fully about it elsewhere.[1] For now it must be said that a powerful case can be made for the Christian belief in the resurrection of the body. This does not imply that the "old" body is, by some miracle, "brought back from the dead." Rather, it says that the essential person, the personality, the spirit, survives death and subsequently expresses itself in a new resurrection body—a body perfectly designed by God for life in the new world of heaven, just as our present bodies are perfectly designed for life on earth.

It makes a big difference in our attitude toward the death of a loved one if we believe that death is the end of their body, but *not the end of them*. I remember as a young man looking down at my father's body in its coffin and thinking, "It looks like Dad, but he's not there." Many, many people have said similar things to me since then. They have seen the body of a loved one, yet have felt that it was "empty"— not just lifeless, but uninhabited. The individual they have known and loved is simply not there. What they are aware of is the absence of the person, even though the familiar form is before their eyes. In a book I have quoted already, Christopher Leach describes viewing his eleven-year-old son's body in the funeral home:

> This shape in the coffin, shaped like my son, was not
> my son. It was an almost perfect statue; or a very skillful
> ventriloquist's dummy: one that would never speak
> . . . What I was looking at was a container for life. The

shell. That which had made Jonathan my son, and your brother, had gone. The flame was out. The light had died. The bird had flown.

That is a common experience, here powerfully described. Leach goes on to ask, but not to answer, the most important question of all: *Where* has the bird flown?

The Bible, in one of its most pessimistic, even cynical books, gives a clear-cut answer: "The spirit returns to God who gave it."[2]

The "bird" has flown, but is not destroyed. The spirit— the "real" person—has returned to God, and will, according to the New Testament, be clothed in a new body, one which will not age, wither, or decay, but will live with God forever. It is that knowledge that gives death a whole new dimension. As the old Latin hymn puts it:

Henceforth is death
But the gate to life immortal.

So, faced with the reality of death, a Christian response has two main elements. The first is acceptance of the inevitable: the body dies. That particular combination of matter completes its role and is destined for disintegration. It may be hard to accept, but sooner or later we have to do so. The container is empty. The shell has no kernel of life. The bird has flown.

But overriding that acceptance of death in the physical sense is the second element, a complementary faith in life. The container or the shell may be empty, but what it once housed now lives elsewhere. The end of the body is not the end of the person. As St. Paul put it: "The perishable must clothe itself with the imperishable, and the mortal with immortality."[3]

However, this fact does not necessarily support the idea of a detachable soul. The Bible does not teach that human

beings *have* a soul if by that we mean some invisible com-
partment or element in the body which survives death, a
"ghost in the human machine." Rather, it teaches that man
is a soul—a unity of physical and spiritual. What survives
death is not a fraction of the whole, but the reality behind
the whole, what the Bible calls the "spirit of man." It is,
in modern language, the personality that transcends death,
the real, essential person, that which makes each individual
distinctive. Death does destroy the body, but it is powerless
to destroy personality. That—Christians believe—is beyond
its destructive touch. Personality lives on, and will do so
forever.

It is impossible to talk about the Christian understanding
of death without considering the death of Jesus. Christians
believe that Jesus is the Son of God and shares God's nature.
But they also believe that he shared human nature. He
was born; he grew up through childhood and adolescence
to manhood. He worked as a carpenter in Nazareth. *And
he died.* God, in the person of his Son, experienced this,
the coldest and darkest thing in human existence. No one
in the chilling grip of bereavement, or even in the twilight
days of a terminal illness, can say that God does not understand.

But it goes farther than that. The death of Jesus was, in
medical terms, "normal." His body was broken by crucifix-
ion and its vital functions ceased. Yet his death is seen by
Christians as a triumph rather than a disaster. By dying,
he conquered death. His own last words, "It is finished,"
were a cry not of despair, as might be supposed, but of
accomplishment: "It is *completed*." He had done what he
came to do.

The resurrection confirmed this. "It was," as St. Peter
explained on the day of Pentecost, "impossible for death

to keep its hold on him . . . He was not abandoned to the grave, nor did his body see decay. God has raised this Jesus to life."[4] The death of Jesus was an essential part of what the early Christians called the "victory over death": "Death has been swallowed up in victory."[5]

In one sense, the death of Jesus gives everyone's death a new dignity and meaning. If God could use death to redeem mankind and bring us eternal life, then death itself cannot be regarded as grotesque, sordid, or evil. Its circumstances are sometimes all those things. But its meaning has been transformed. It is not a pointless experience of pain, either for the dying person or for those who mourn him, but an event dignified by God himself, and given purpose, meaning, and hope in the death of Jesus.

3

THE HEALING FUNERAL

I REMEMBER THE FIRST FUNERAL I ever attended. I think I was ten. A girl in our school, in a remote village in the Welsh mountains, had died. We were all led from our classes across the road to the churchyard to take part in the service. There was no notion, in that wonderfully raw and realistic community, that children should be shielded from the presence of death. The white stone cottages of the village huddled around the graveyard, as though wanting to enfold the dead in the bosom of the community. Life and death were each a part of the pattern of existence— as indivisible from each other as the cloud-capped hills were from the cloud-filled sky.

Twenty or thirty of us stood around the grave, behind the weeping parents and relatives. Just before the little coffin was lowered into the grave we sang a Welsh hymn. It was about Jesus the Good Shepherd and his lambs, and by the last line everyone was in tears, including most of us children. I still remember the stillness in the churchyard, the wet grass, and the pale, tear-stained faces. I went back to the village last year and found the grave, and on the stone marking it were a few words of that hymn we sang all those years ago.

Since then I have been to many funerals. A few, those for people particularly close to me, are etched in my memory. Many are less distinct. One or two I can hardly recall. Yet I know every one of them was moving. And the two funerals at which I have preached have been unusually emotional experiences.

For many reasons bereaved people often are apprehensive about the funeral. After all, it is on this occasion that their private grief becomes public. They know they will have to face people—not just close relatives, but also comparative strangers such as colleagues or distant relatives of the deceased person. And they will have to endure that most heart-rending of all moments when the coffin containing the body of their loved one finally disappears from sight. For most people it is at this moment that the fact of death becomes a stark reality. Not only has the bird flown; the cage is also being destroyed.

However, often in retrospect bereaved persons can regard the funeral as a healing aid to recovery—I know that the funerals of my own parents were very important to me in coping with bereavement, and helped me realize how valuable the ritual is, however distasteful it may seem beforehand. This ceremony is perhaps the first step in the process of accepting the death of a loved one and moving on from bitterness or anger to the deep unjudging grief without which healing cannot come.

It is fascinating to note that funerals are apparently the first religious ceremonies of the human race. We can see in drawings on cave walls and in the evidence at ancient burial sites that our earliest forefathers honored their dead and committed them to some further existence—an existence they didn't understand but still hoped for.

So we can see that it is our nature to regard the death of a fellow human being as significant, and to mark it with ritual and ceremony. The specific rites have varied enormously, but have always involved disposing of the body in a way that would signify passage—movement *on*, rather than simply disappearance. The funeral ships of the Vikings, drifting out to sea in a blaze of flame, were seen as the passage to Valhalla. The coins buried with the dead of the ancient Mediterranean world were to be used to pay the ferryman for the journey across the water to the shadowy land of the dead. The pyramid tombs of ancient Egypt enclosed not only the corpse, but also food and amusement for the life hereafter. In the Muslim funeral, the body is buried in a sitting position facing Mecca, anticipating the resurrection.

And in the Christian funeral, the body is committed to earth or to fire, but the spirit is committed to God who made it, "in sure and certain hope of the resurrection to eternal life." It is a service of departure but not disappearance, of parting but not finality. It is a ritual of grief, but not hopeless grief.

There is no reason to fear the funeral. Often the bereaved person gains great strength from the people who come to the service. It encourages us when we see that our sense of sorrow and deprivation is shared by many others. The funeral often helps, too, by ritualizing our grief, containing its raw edges within a familiar, measured form, and at the same time bringing it out into the open to be shared.

The Jewish community can teach us something about mourning. Their mourning period, or *shiva*, lasts a week. During this time prayers are said, and the grieving persons are expected to spend their time talking to visitors about the dead person. Family and friends are present with the bereaved, not so much comforting them as sharing in their mourning. Less orthodox Jews have adopted a one-day *shiva*, but this has been found less effective because it does not allow time and space for the vital process of public grieving.

I am not saying that a seven-day funeral for Christians is necessary. However, I do think the period leading up to and immediately following the funeral is an extremely important time for the bereaved, and handling it well can greatly aid their recovery. Talking about the dead person (rather than tactfully ignoring the subject), and sharing the experience of grief with family and friends are two very constructive ways to use that time.

Very often the real grieving begins at or after the funeral. I cannot stress too much that this grief must not be resisted, repressed, or despised—in ourselves or in others. The traditional "stiff upper lip" is completely out of place at a funeral. If someone feels like crying, then by all means let him cry. The tears of one person (especially a male) may help to release the tears of others. Societies that know how to grieve have far fewer problems with bereavement than those that regard a public show of grief as undignified, if not cowardly. There is nothing cowardly about shedding tears for the loss of someone we love, but there *is* something cowardly about repressing them, or keeping them private, for fear of what others will think.

Some people argue that Christians, believing in the resurrection of the dead, should not grieve over those who have died. Rather, they should see the funeral as a kind of celebration or thanksgiving, suffused with hope. They may quote St. Paul writing to the church at Thessalonica: "We do not want you . . . to grieve about those who die, like the rest of men, who have no hope." Or they may echo the apostle's own hope that he might soon die and go to be with Christ, "which is far better." Should not Christians, then, rejoice at death as the gateway to eternal life? And is not grief a denial of our faith and an expression of doubt about the faith of the person who has died?

We can answer that certainly thanksgiving, and even celebration, are present in a Christian funeral. Services in all the great traditions reflect this note of hope: "I am the resurrection and the life, says the Lord. He who believes in me will live, even though he dies; and whoever lives and believes in me will never die." So begins the Anglican funeral service. At the Second Vatican Council the Roman Catholic Church ordered that the vestments worn at funerals should no longer be the black ones of mourning and sorrow, but the white Easter vestments of celebration. Hope, based on God's promises, is indeed the underlying principle of a Christian funeral.

But that is not the same as saying that grieving and tears should have no part in bereavement. After all, the same Jesus who made that confident assertion about immortality—"he who lives and believes in me will never die"—was within a few minutes weeping at the tomb of his friend Lazarus. He knew all about resurrection, new life, and immortality. But he also knew about human love, about sympathy and separation. Lazarus was soon to be raised to life again, but there before Jesus' eyes were all the sad trappings of human mortality—the weeping mourners, the distraught relatives, and the dark tomb. It would take a cold heart to remain unmoved in the face of so much sorrow.

But more than that, the death of a loved one is a separation, as real a parting as if he or she had gone to live on the other side of the world—indeed, *more* real. There will be no letters, phone calls, or holiday reunions. If tears are appropriate at the airport (and they are) then surely they are appropriate at the graveside. The parting of death is real, total, and (in this life) irreversible. Our faith that we shall see our loved ones again does not eliminate our grief at that parting, though it does take away the hopelessness that would turn it into despair.

I believe that St. Paul was condemning despair ("grieving like the rest of men, who have no hope") but not grief of this sympathetic kind, the grief that Jesus expressed at the tomb of Lazarus. Tears of sadness and tears of despair may look the same, but their sources are different. When the Christian elders wept as they said goodbye to the apostle Paul at Miletus, they had not stopped believing in the resurrection. They were not in despair. But they knew that never again on earth would they see this man whom they loved so much and who had meant so much to them, and that was "what grieved them."[1]

So the Christian must not resist or suppress a proper sorrow at the parting death brings. Grief is not a denial of faith, nor does it contradict a proper note of thanksgiving and even celebration in a funeral. I have wept at funerals, yet also shared in this sense of triumph. So we say our sad and tearful goodbyes, and sing our hymns of resurrection—there is no contradiction between the two.

The funeral service itself is a good opportunity to clarify these issues. If it is approached and conducted properly, the service will do three things. First, it will signify, in a ceremonial way, the fact of death. In a booklet on the clergyman's approach to these services, an Anglican rector writes that the funeral should encourage the mourners "to face the fact that death is final, to let the dead person go, and not to cling to them in spiritualism, in graveside worship for years after, in keeping their room undisturbed . . . We should be prepared to pay the price of more open grief during and immediately after the service, if it will help to avoid the denial of death and to encourage people to seek help and strength afresh from Christ for the future rather than from a vague communion with the past."[2] This is the most difficult part of the funeral for the closest relatives and friends, but it may be the most immediately helpful. It *is* a service of farewell.

The visible sign of this farewell, the burial or cremation of the body, is often the moment when suppressed grief emerges. This moment of farewell should not be avoided. In fact, a bereaved person who refuses to attend the funeral is actually hurting himself. Painful as it is, seeing the body "go" is an important part of the process of healing and eventual recovery.

Some people are unsure about the validity of cremation. They feel that it shows less respect for the body, that it provides no lasting memorial, and even that it contradicts the Christian belief in resurrection. Such strong doubts cannot be dismissed as trivial or superstitious. After all, the Roman Catholic Church was officially opposed to cremation on very much those grounds until quite recently.

Nevertheless, these fears are groundless. The practice of burning the remains of the dead has a long and honorable history; it is hard to see how cremation could be considered less reverent than consigning the body to the earth. Sooner or later, in both cases, the body is destroyed, its elements converted into other forms. Cremation leaves no grave or tomb which can be visited, but that may even be a good thing. Sometimes a grave, too frequently visited or decked with flowers, becomes a handicap to a bereaved person, making it more difficult for him to accept the reality of his loss. After all, there is nothing there, just as nothing is left after a cremation. All that is valuable, immortal, spiritual has gone elsewhere, and lives on in a new realm. This is why cremation is irrelevant to any discussion about resurrection—or is it suggested that people whose bodies are destroyed in accidental fires, or by war bombs, are thereby denied any possibility of resurrection? *How* we dispose of the body is unimportant, as long as it is done with dignity and respect for the body, which is God's handiwork. That we *do* dispose of it is an inevitable part of the process of bereavement.

In addition to the fact of death, the funeral service ceremonially expresses, secondly, our appreciation for the person who has died and our respect for the dignity of mankind. The body that lies in the coffin is treated with reverence as the mortal remains of an immortal spirit. But it also represents the memories of someone we have loved and cherished, perhaps for many years. These memories, and our appreciation and respect, are expressed in prayers, psalms, and hymns, and counterbalance that sharper note of the reality of death that also runs through the service.

The third element expressed in a Christian funeral is the church's faith in the resurrection. We are an Easter people. From first to last, our acceptance of the reality of death and our thanksgiving for a life well lived are shot through with our faith in the risen Jesus. The parting is real, but not final. The life completed on earth, which we commemorate, is continued and fulfilled in the life eternal. We grieve, but not, in St. Paul's words, "without hope."

I said that a properly conducted service will include these elements. Sadly, one has to add that there are some funerals in which they are hard to find. Increasingly, funeral services and committals are taking place at the cemetery or crematorium chapel and are being conducted by a minister who knows neither the mourners nor the deceased.

This *can* be avoided. Every person has the right to a funeral service in his own church, conducted by his own minister, though the funeral director may not mention this possibility to the family—perhaps because relatively few people ask for it, or because it complicates the normal routine. However, if the family, or the one who has died, has had any kind of Christian beliefs, it is completely reasonable for the bereaved persons to ask for, and if necessary, to insist on, a church service followed by committal at the crematorium or cemetery.

If there is to be a church service, then normally the minister will discuss with the family the choice of hymns and perhaps Bible readings. It is often a matter of genuine satisfaction for the relatives when they can be involved in these details of the service.

Obviously a service in the cemetery chapel conducted by a stranger is less satisfactory, but very often the minister makes a real effort to meet the needs of the mourners, possibly by talking with them for a few minutes before the service or after the committal.

In any case, the inherent seriousness and momentousness of the occasion will create a setting in which the mourners can, if they wish, give thanks for the life well lived, acknowledge the reality of the parting of death, and celebrate their faith in the resurrection. I have never seen a funeral service so badly or unfeelingly conducted that it completely obscured these three principles.

After the funeral, by tradition, there is a family get-together. This is a splendid tradition, rooted in social and psychological need, and is almost always a very encouraging occasion. In the hubbub of family conversation and the excitement of long-separated relatives meeting again, loved ones who have died are not so much overlooked as absorbed. This was their environment, their setting. These people were their flesh and blood. Here they were at home. Silence would be inappropriate, as would gloom or despair. There may not be much laughter, but there should be warmth and life, a celebration of family solidarity in the face of its most unrelenting foe.

4

GETTING BACK
TO NORMAL

TIME, WE ARE TOLD, is the great healer. There is some truth in that saying, but it's also true that time's healing leaves scars and pressure points which can break down or flare up unexpectedly long after the painful event. And while time's healing is slow, it is not necessarily gradual: it can proceed by leaps and bounds, then regress as suddenly as it advanced.

In the early days of a bereavement, when friends and relatives are most supportive, the healing of grief may appear rapid and successful. The bereaved person seems to be coping very well. There is a lot to do, and decisions and plans to make, so that the wounded mind is shielded from those empty, blank moments of loneliness and deprivation that are the seedbeds of negative grief. It is *after* the hustle and bustle of the funeral that the slow process of acceptance begins, and often the low point is reached some months later.

The majority of severe problems seem to occur between six months and two years after bereavement. "It is important," writes one authority, "that we remain sensitive to the needs of the bereaved for much longer than we usually do. Only gradually does acceptance come, the adjustment to drastic and far-reaching loss taking place slowly. When the death is sudden the shock can persist for much longer."

The two enemies of recovery are loneliness and deprivation. It is wise to recognize them for what they are. If the bereaved person has lost a constant companion—a spouse, a roommate, a close and valued confidant—then the loneliness can be like physical pain. He will catch himself commenting on something during a television program, or pointing out a rare bird in the garden or a person passing on the street, but there is no one listening, no one with whom to share the experience. These are the moments when it hurts most—the cold sudden *realization* of loss.

Familiar rooms and places, mutually shared pleasures, favorite haunts—these seem to offer a way back to past joys but can suddenly overwhelm one with disappointment. A person who is recovering can suffer a totally unexpected setback through being caught unawares by a person, a place, or a situation. It is difficult, and often impossible, to avoid such circumstances completely, but it is wise to beware of them. Sometimes a vacation away at a relative's or friend's home can help, but the familiar setting still has to be faced eventually, and faced without the loved companion.

Particularly difficult are small things—events, anniversaries—that would hardly be known to anyone else. They can lead to bad days, and bad days brooded on can lead to bad weeks and months. A letter addressed to the dead person, perhaps an annual reminder, can catch us with our defenses down.

The psychological answer is to learn distraction, the trick

of thinking about other things at such moments of danger. Such willpower is not fail-safe but the degree to which the mind can be disciplined away from certain areas and into others is surprising. Prayer is a very valuable part of this process for the Christian, and it can help in several different ways.

In itself, prayer can be an answer to loneliness. In one sense the person who prays is never alone. Jesus promised that his Father in heaven would hear and answer every prayer offered in his name. Many lonely people have come to know the presence of God through prayer, and that presence has so pervaded their day-to-day experience that they can honestly say they are never alone.

It is also true that praying about a problem can transform it, perhaps even into something that brings joy. If, in our conversations with God, we tell him about our fears and hurts, and ask for his help for the times when we are suddenly overwhelmed with sorrow, he will help us to have confidence in him. Then, when the crises come, our feelings at their base can be positive rather than negative and we can see the painful times as within God's will in a larger, more long-term sense.

A third value of prayer to the grieving person is its re-minder of the communion of saints. Prayer for or about someone else binds us to them and creates or strengthens our concept of unity with them in the created order under God. For the bereaved person this idea can be helpful. Recalling the lost loved one and praying about him encour-ages the bereaved person to realize that they are still bound to each other because they are both bound to God. In chapter five I shall return to the subject of prayer for, with, or about the dead, but for now it will suffice to say that prayer can counter loneliness by reminding us not only of the presence of God, but also of the continuing link that believers have through him with those who have died.

So, prayer can help to offset loneliness. But for most people it needs to be supplemented by or grounded in the support of friends. Loneliness is not, for the bereaved, the absence of people, but the absence of a person—a specific person who has been a close companion. This person cannot be replaced by an assortment of people taking turns spending time with the one grieving. The greatest help of all is the friend or relative who can give regular, consistent, reliable time and companionship.

This will not be easy. Derek Nuttall writes in the article to which I have already referred:

> We should persist with our offers of help to the bereaved. Grief is a process: moods change and problems fluctuate in their prominence and intensity. We offer help, but on that occasion it is refused, we tend not to repeat it; yet a day or week later the bereaved person may be longing for such an offer. We need to be sensitive to their changing moods—now wanting to be alone, then to have company; now wanting to talk about what has happened, then to sit silent or discuss other things.
>
> We may feel we are intruding, but it is better to err in favor of staying in contact, because other stresses will occur which will cause further grief or reopen wounds.

These are wise words. It is easy to be upset by the unpredictability of a bereaved person, or to take offense at his sudden wish to be left alone. The role of a friend is not to argue or be resentful, however; it is to be available. "You know where I am. Give me a call—or I'll drop in tomorrow anyway." Tomorrow things may be different. Our company and support may be not only needed, but wanted—two very different things. We must not give the bereaved person any excuse for feeling deserted or let down by those nearest him, even if our pride does take a few mild knocks in the process. *Being there*, or close by, is the important thing.

We should also watch for symptoms of morbid introspection. Internal loneliness is a bitter and corrosive thing. It can lead a bereaved person to become something of a recluse, unwilling to go out and meet people or even to be seen in public. He may plead illness, or claim that his appearance is horrible or that people will talk about him. Here a close friend can be invaluable in easing him back into normal social contacts a step at a time—perhaps first planning a shopping trip or a visit to church. Slowly, the intricate pattern of day-to-day relationships can be rebuilt without the loved one who had previously played an indispensable part in that pattern. This is a difficult task, and we should not underestimate the challenge it presents. It's hard to begin rebuilding close relationships when we are still suffering from the effects of a bereavement. We don't feel like risking our feelings again. Much like one who has suffered a broken engagement, we are the wounded party, and we're reluctant to put ourselves in the position of being hurt a second time. But friendships, and less intimate ordinary contacts, must be rebuilt if life is to return to anything approaching normality.

Some, far from becoming recluses, try to fend off internal loneliness with desperate busyness, driving themselves to their physical limits with relentless activity. This is just as dangerous. It too is a response to deprivation, an attempt to stave off the pressing awareness of loss, by filling every available minute, from morning to bedtime, with bustle and work. Very often this leads to physical or nervous collapse.

Again, friends must watch out for the symptoms and

help the bereaved person achieve a sensible balance of activity. This is certainly easier said than done. It's seldom helpful to volunteer to take over some of the person's tasks. The best solution is to provide intervals in the cycle of activity, times when you can sit down together and do something more relaxing, such as playing cards, talking, or watching television. Taking a walk together is another good alternative. The bereaved person will not readily do these things on his own because they are the kind of activities that leave the mind free to remember, and that is what he fears most.

For Christians, the slow process of recovery from loss includes an effort to start practicing their faith as they had in the past. Their prayer, Bible reading, and churchgoing probably have declined or even lapsed altogether over the traumatic days of early bereavement. A further obstacle may be that the person who previously provided company, and often motivation, in these activities is no longer available. A prayer partner may have been lost, as well as a husband, wife, sibling, or friend.

Here is where friends, or one close friend, can be a great help. A simple offer to pray together, without pressure, can break through the barrier of hesitancy and fear. Similarly, an invitation to read the Bible together, or to join a small home study group, may motivate the grieving person to resume Bible reading. And certainly a friend's offer to accompany him to church—and to keep up the practice for as long as it is desired—can make all the difference. Bereaved people often have a quite irrational fear of meeting people, or perhaps of being watched or assessed, which inhibits their return to church. It can be reinforced by the awkwardness or embarrassment with which church members sometimes face them, not sure whether to talk about the death or ignore it.

There is no doubt that this first encounter between a bereaved person and his wider circle of friends and acquaintances (a church congregation is an excellent sample) does present problems. Some members of the congregation will handle the situation with a burst of irrelevant bonhomie, talking loudly and cheerily about everything except the topic and the person which everyone knows must be uppermost in their minds. Others adopt a reverential tone, dropping their voices and approaching the bereaved person with an exaggerated delicacy. Still others try to be "normal"—but the fact is that the situation is *not* normal.

A big danger for the friends of a bereaved person is that they will worry about how they should approach their hurting friend. Such worry has an embarrassing way of communicating itself. The person who has been bereaved is the same friend or acquaintance as he was before the event. The bereaved are not suffering from some contagious disease, nor have they been transformed into psychological freaks. They do not expect their bereavement to be the sole topic of conversation, but neither do they expect it to be ignored. *They* cannot ignore it, so why should their friends?

In practice, a normal, friendly approach—including whatever gesture of greeting you would usually offer them —should be supplemented by a simple assurance of your understanding and sympathy. Some phrase such as "We've been thinking of you" is enough to put the rest of your conversation with them into context. A genuine interest in their family comings and goings, any appropriate offers of help, even in small things like transportation, shopping, and household chores, and a willingness to *listen:* these are the positive ingredients friends can contribute to the process of rebuilding a normal social life. Those who have experienced bereavement themselves can also add that most reassuring of all statements, "I understand how you are feeling."

Death is normal. It is not some freak occurrence that afflicts the odd one or two, but a universal experience of mankind. It is solidarity with the bereaved that will strengthen them most of all. The path through bereavement to recovery is a well-trod one, and those who have already walked it have the most to offer those who are finding the going heavy.

As time goes on, the process of returning to normality changes. The initial difficulty of taking up ordinary life, meeting friends and neighbors, resuming day-to-day activities leads on into the much longer process of readjustment. Sometimes those who cope very well with the initial stage run into severe problems later, often because they are unaware of the challenges to be faced as time goes on.

For example, clearing the personal belongings and effects of a loved one can be a very traumatic experience. Few people tackle it immediately, and it can often be left for a long while. But sooner or later it has to be done and it can cause unexpected feelings of grief. Clothes, papers, books, a wallet or handbag, a cherished memento, a letter—any of these can rekindle memories and start the tears flowing.

This is not necessarily a bad thing, provided we are ready for it, half expecting it. If we are caught unaware, it can knock us out of our stride. Sometimes we find out something completely unexpected, perhaps something about ourselves, or something that causes us guilt, jealousy, or resentment. Few of us welcome anyone, even a loved one, rummaging through our pockets or handbag. It is a peculiarly intrusive thing to do, almost a violation of privacy. So, if one feels particularly sensitive about this task, it may be wise to invite a trusted friend or executor to go through the personal effects, simply referring to the bereaved person anything that requires a decision.

Anniversaries and birthdays can also stir up memories. It is probably better to anticipate them than to allow them to creep up on us. Indeed, a positive approach—making the day special in some way, perhaps by inviting a few friends or relatives to a meal, or having an outing—can remove the sting before it strikes.

Some find a visit to the cemetery or memorial a help, and, provided it is not unbearably painful, this can be a positive gesture of remembrance and reflection. However, visiting the grave should not be seen as a duty or obligation, nor a failure to do so as a failure of love. In the deepest sense, there is nobody there. Our loved one is no longer bound by mortality. As the angels said to the disciples on the first Easter morning, "He is not here. He is risen."

The most difficult long-term adjustment involves living in the changed circumstances that death creates. In some cases the main wage earner has died and the resulting economic circumstances are painful. In other cases an elderly parent who has occupied much time and attention for many years has died, leaving the bereaved person with lots of empty time. Changes like these are difficult at the best of times. Following bereavement, they can loom ahead like menacing mountains.

There is no easy answer, but it is safe to say that changes are better faced one by one than *en masse*. If it is necessary to relocate, then it is probably best to avoid any other major changes at the same time. But where there are drastic, long-term financial changes, one may not be able to go slowly. They may simply have to be faced, with advice from reliable friends.

If a son or daughter suddenly finds a lot of time on his or her hands, the temptation may be to quickly take on too much. It is not usually wise to make decisions in the immediate aftermath of an emotional upheaval. Later on the alternatives can be more carefully assessed, with less likelihood of making serious mistakes.

In any case death leads to change for those who are left behind. Life has to be reorganized without a person who was an important part of it. Many of us who are into or beyond our middle years do not relish change even at the best of times, and particularly when it is thrust on us against our will. But death's changes are inevitable, so it is useless to fight them.

Again, a positive approach is best. Fear of change is almost always worse than the change itself. The Christian can look to the unchanging nature of God, to whom we are inextricably linked and upon whom our lives are built. Jesus Christ, the Bible tells us, is "the same yesterday, today, and forever." Whatever changes affect the pattern of our lives or our circumstances, we who trust in him have a fixed reference point upon which we can rely. We can see the changes, therefore, as within God's will for us, and the circumstances they create as another area of experience that he will share with us.

5

QUESTIONS PEOPLE ASK

INEVITABLY, DEATH RAISES QUESTIONS in people's minds, and some of those questions are religious ones. Even devout Christians who have never questioned their belief in "the resurrection of the body, and the life everlasting" find themselves facing questions and doubts about their dead loved one.

Is death the end? It certainly looks like it as we gaze down at a lifeless body. Will we ever again see the person who has died? And if so, where, when, and how? Will we recognize him? Will he be a spirit or ghost rather than a real, whole person? Does he know about us now—can he pray for us and take an interest in our day-to-day lives? Or is he divided from us, even if only temporarily, by some impenetrable barrier raised by death? Can we—*should* we— pray for him, or about him? And what does that phrase "the communion of saints" mean?

In one sense many of these questions are unanswerable because no human being has firsthand experience of life beyond death. We may express opinions and beliefs, and

at the same time fear that these beliefs are merely a reflection of our wishes. In the end, we must conclude that the
only reliable information we have about these matters
comes to us from beyond our own experience.

The only convincing instance in history of a person rising
from the dead—as distinct from a temporary recovery—is
that of Jesus. Clever people have done their best for nearly
two thousand years to discredit this account. Yet today it
is probably more reasonable, according to the evidence, to
believe that Jesus rose from the dead than that he did not.[1]

Jesus' death was no inconspicuous event. His followers'
claim that he had risen from the dead was broadcast in
the streets of Jerusalem during a religious festival. The rival
Jewish and Roman authorities had everything to gain by
disproving this claim, and it should have been an easy
matter to discredit the idea that a man had come back from
the dead. Yet they never could.

The Christian church grew and more and more people
accepted the unlikely proposition that its crucified founder
was still alive, but the silence of the opposition was deafen-
ing. Apart from hints that the body of Jesus might have
been removed by his followers and a suggestion that his
miracles were the work of the Prince of Evil, history records
no evidence contrary to the extraordinary claim that Jesus
rose from the dead. The very disciples who were alleged
to have stolen his body were prepared to die for the truth
of his resurrection—a strange contradiction! With mount-
ing conviction, much of the Mediterranean world of the
first century, a cynical, philosophical kind of world, accepted the resurrection of Jesus.

So one man conquered death, and returned to tell us
about it: not in detail, but in principle. If we want to find
satisfying answers to our questions about life beyond death,

we cannot do better than listen to what Jesus and the apostles whom he instructed had to say about it. Theirs is the only firsthand, reliable testimony we have, and the New Testament the only authoritative guide on the subject.

Is death the end?

Broadly speaking, history indicates three basic views on the subject of life beyond death. Some people have always believed that death is the end. They see human life as a brief and finite thing, death being like the extinguishing of a candle. The light goes out and there is nothing. This idea is as old as human history. Mentioned even in the Old Testament, it was a widely held belief among the Jews of the Second Temple period when Jesus lived; one of the two main groups of theologians of his day, the Sadducees, denied any notion of a resurrection or afterlife. This was also the belief of the Stoics, one of the period's two important schools of Greek philosophy. Today, a number of people hold this view.

The second view is that a dead person lives on in some discarnate way (without any form or substance) in the minds and memories of those who have loved him. This is a kind of "survival," and some of those who hold this view would go so far as to say that memory of the deceased can be so powerful as to create visual images (visions), sounds, and sensations that may convince those closest to the dead person that he is still alive and communicating with them.

The third view is that after this life human beings are translated to a new and better life. Considering how unlikely this view appears when we evaluate it according to the evidence of our senses, it's remarkable what a hold the idea has had on our race from the dawn of history. By far the greater part of humankind has always believed in a life beyond death, variously interpreted, from the Valhalla of the Vikings to the Elysian Fields of the Romans.

While the Christian belief in resurrection is based on this same conviction that death is not the end, it is far removed from the common understanding of the life "beyond" as simply a replay of earthly existence minus the handicaps. For the Christian, the life beyond death is a new life. This "life eternal," as Jesus called it, takes place in the completely different environment of heaven, in a new bodily vehicle perfectly suited for life there. Its relationship to this life and the resurrection body's relationship to the earthly body are likened by St. Paul to the relationship between a seed buried in the ground and the plant that grows from it.[2] In both cases there is a continuity of the life, but a total transformation of its vehicle. Like a moth developing from a caterpillar, the human spirit, released from the confines of earth, is free to enter a new realm of existence.

This is what the Bible means when it talks about eternal life— not just life that goes on forever, but the kind of life that shares the eternal nature of God. There really can be no doubt that Jesus believed in this eternal life and promised it to those who believed in him: "God so loved the world that he gave his one and only Son, that whoever believes in him shall not perish but have eternal life."[3]

This belief, central to the teaching of Jesus and the early church, was enshrined in the oldest creeds: "I believe in the resurrection of the body and the life everlasting." This does not mean, as some have wrongly supposed, that Christians believe in the restoration of the body that has died. That body is finished at death, and is laid aside with reverence. It has no future. The phrase in the creed means that the resurrection is "bodily." We will not live on as ghosts or spirits, but as people, expressing our new life through new, transformed bodies. The life in these bodies will have a continuity with our present life, but the vehicle will be completely new. "God gives them a body," as St. Paul put it, a body suitable for life in the spiritual realm, heaven, where he is.[4]

That life is *real* life. It is not the shadowy existence of a spirit world. Jesus called it "life in all its fullness."[5] St. Paul described it as "far better" than the life we know on earth. The testimony of the New Testament, reflected in the creeds of the church through the centuries, is clear about this: there is life beyond the grave.

Who is raised?

It is one thing to say that there is life beyond death. However, it is another thing to say that everyone has the right to that life. Many bereaved people do not find much comfort in the knowledge that heaven exists, because they are unsure whether the person whose death they mourn was qualified to go there. The person may have had no religious beliefs at all, or perhaps moral flaws in his character or behavior made the state of his inner person unclear to outsiders. He may have been conspicuously irreligious. Can we brush aside all of this? Or, more importantly, does God brush it aside?

Sadly, we find no claim that heaven awaits everyone. The Bible clearly states that entrance to heaven is on the grounds of moral perfection—which would seem to exclude all of us! But the New Testament also teaches that the sacrifice of Jesus on the cross makes it possible for us to be forgiven our sins. We can enter heaven on the grounds of his moral excellence, not our own: "God made [Jesus] to be sin for us, so that in him we might become the righteousness of God."[6]

I believe the Bible is also clear that every human being "survives" death, and that after this life we are answerable for what we have done during it. In the book at the end of the New Testament called The Revelation to John, the writer records his remarkable vision of the "last things," telling us that he saw:

> . . . a great white throne and him who was seated on it . . . And I saw the dead, great and small, standing before the throne, and books were opened. Another book was opened, which is the book of life. The dead were judged according to what they had done as recorded in the books. The sea gave up the dead that were in it, and death and Hades gave up the dead that were in them, and each person was judged according to what he had done.[7]

For anyone unfamiliar with this kind of visionary writing, Revelation is a notoriously difficult book to understand. Even for people who have studied the book carefully, it is dangerous to make dogmatic pronouncements based on the metaphorical language. The powerful imagery simply cannot be reduced to the kind of propositions upon which twentieth-century people like to make their decisions of behavior and belief.

Nevertheless, Revelation reflects the beliefs of the church in the apostolic era about the "last things." What the writer says, through his imagery and allegories, is consistent with what St. Paul says in his closely reasoned arguments on the subject,[8] and also with the hints that Jesus gave on the few occasions when he spoke about the ultimate destiny of human beings. It is probably best not to push conclusions too far—those who profess to find in the Bible a detailed plan for the future of this planet and the destiny of each human being are usually guilty of reading too much into visions and images that were not given for that purpose and were never intended to be used in so literal and arbitrary a way. I believe that the early Christians, conforming to the teachings of Jesus and the apostles, saw the nature of judgment and life after death in the following way.

First, death and judgment are common to every person. "Man is destined to die once, and after that to face judgment."[9] God's justice demands that the injustices of life be put right. Indeed, if he did not require this, he would be either unjust (which contradicts his holiness) or incapable (which contradicts his omnipotence).

Secondly, this judgment is based on God's moral law, the basic principles of which are laid down in the Ten Commandments given through Moses and summarized by Jesus: "You shall love the Lord your God with all your heart, mind, soul, and strength, and your neighbor as yourself." This law, St. Paul argues, is found not only in these biblical formulas; it is so fundamental that even those who "do not have the law" can find this law "written on their hearts," and so they are, in his memorable phrase, "a law for themselves."[10] He means that any human being can and should revere his Creator, and can and should behave in a way that he instinctively knows will please that Creator. Consequently, he argues, everyone is under God's judgment: "All have sinned and fall short of the glory of God." [11] The books mentioned in John's vision may well be the books of the Law, by which the actions of those about to be assessed will be judged.

Thirdly, it is possible, through the grace of God and the death and resurrection of Jesus, for men and women to be forgiven for their failure to live by God's moral standards, and to be justified, that is, regarded as though they had never sinned. Jesus did not die for his own sins, but for the sin of the world. Through his death we can be restored to a new relationship with the Father. The names of those who are thus restored are, in the visionary language of John, "written in the book of life." They are not subject to judgment or condemnation; after death their life's work is assessed and rewarded.

Fourthly, those who have not had the opportunity to respond to the good news about Jesus, and those who have lived all their lives in what St. Paul would have called "pagan darkness," all the while responding to whatever divine light was given them and seeking (however imperfectly) to follow the unwritten law of God in their hearts, will be judged fairly and mercifully by a just and generous God. This seems to me to be the meaning of a rather tortuous passage in Paul's letter to the church at Rome:

> When Gentiles [i.e. "pagans," unbelievers, people without the revelation of God], who do not have the law, do by nature things required by the law, they are a law for themselves, even though they do not have the law, since they show that the requirements of the law are written on their hearts, their consciences also bearing witness, and their thoughts now accusing, now even defending them. This will take place on the day when God will judge men's secrets through Jesus Christ, as my gospel declares.[12]

These ideas help to answer the question, "Who goes to heaven?" Everyone is raised from the dead and judged by God. Those who have believed in Jesus Christ, and have therefore received God's forgiveness, are accepted without question. Of those who have not had such faith in Jesus, one must distinguish between those who have never heard the gospel, or heard it only in an incomplete or distorted form, and those who have heard it and have consciously rejected it. The former group will be judged by God on the basis of how they have lived in response to whatever divine light has been given them. The latter group, those who have rejected God's love, can now have no complaints if they find themselves rejected from heaven.

But one can be absolutely certain that God will be completely fair to everyone. "Shall not the Judge of all the earth do right?" All that we learn of God in the Bible, and through his Son, Jesus, tells us that he is merciful—his nature is always to have mercy. He takes no pleasure in seeing a single one of his creatures rejected. "He is patient with you, not wanting anyone to perish, but everyone to come to repentance."[13] We may be sure, where our loved ones are concerned, that God will not judge them harshly. He loves them, in spite of all their faults, even more than we do. It is only those who exercise their own moral freedom to reject his love who are excluded from his presence—and, it should be noted that God is not the one who excludes them. They exclude themselves.

Is our relationship with loved ones ended at their death?

Probably more commonly expressed than an anxiety about the eternal destiny of a loved one is the fear that we will never see the person again, anywhere. We talk of bereavement, and the word itself expresses the experience: we are bereft of someone, deprived of his company and companionship. This bereavement feels total. It is not like the separation caused by emigration or travel; we know that it is irreversible. One can visit a friend who has moved to the other side of the world. But someone who has gone to the other side of death has moved out of our world forever. It is impossible to exaggerate the loneliness that death can create, and its most bitter element is this irreversibility. As Shakespeare said through the words of Hamlet, death is

> *That undiscovered country from whose bourn*
> *No traveller returns.*

But the Christian hope contradicts this. One traveler *did* return—Jesus. His rising from the dead and his new life are seen by the writers of the Bible as the prototype of all our resurrections: "Because I live, you will also live." And the New Testament clearly testifies that death is now defeated. Its effect on the human body is indeed irreversible, but it has lost its power to destroy the human spirit. The person—the real "you"—will not simply survive death, but will blossom from it into a new and better life in a new and better environment called heaven.

Still, we ask, will we meet our loved ones there? It would be little consolation to know that our parents, husbands, wives, brothers, sisters, friends, and children were living on in some new spiritual world if we couldn't look forward to sharing that experience with them someday. Theories and concepts are small comfort when what we really want more than anything is the beloved *person*.

So, what does the Christian faith teach about this? The reunion with our loved ones figures prominently in some of the more sentimental Victorian hymns:

> *What knitting severed friendships up*
> *Where partings are no more . . .*

or, more triumphantly:

> *Yes, we'll gather at the river,*
> *The beautiful, beautiful river,*
> *That flows through the city of God.*

What does the Bible say? In general, the biblical pictures we are given—and they are pictures, not factual descriptions— all speak of heaven as a place of light and beauty, where innumerable multitudes of people from every race live together in perfect harmony with one another and with God.[14] In heaven there is no sadness, suffering, handicap, or pain, and no death.[15] There are no exclusive relationships to cause envy, jealousy, or disappointment. Past grievances between individuals, groups, and even nations are perfectly healed.[16] And at the center of this vast, united kingdom is the divine Man, Jesus, the object of his people's love and worship, as well as their guide and protector.

Obviously no words in human language could describe an existence which is literally beyond our sphere of understanding, any more than a human fetus could describe what adult life on earth is like, or, for that matter, a caterpillar on a cabbage leaf could describe what life is like for the butterfly soaring in the branches far above his head. We are given glimpses, but that is all. The promise is quite simply that it will be better, and faith takes God at his word.

However, St. Paul did deal with the specific question of our future relationship with lost loved ones, because it had been raised by the Christian church at Thessalonica.[17] The first generations of Christians expected the return of Jesus to be imminent, so at first they probably did not think a great deal about what happens to Christians who die. But as they realized that the return of Jesus could be long delayed, certainly far beyond their lifetime, the matter of the "Christian dead" became a pressing one. They were afraid there might be a divide between those who had died and those who were still alive at the Second Coming. Consequently some people fell into hopeless grief, fearing that they might never meet their loved ones again.

Paul responded to such questions by referring to the ultimate authority. He said that, "according to the Lord's own word" (which presumably means the direct teaching of Jesus to the apostles), those who are still alive at the time of the Lord's coming will "certainly not precede those who have fallen asleep." Indeed, the Christian dead will rise first, and "after that, we who are still alive and are left will be caught up with them in the clouds to meet the Lord in the air. So, we will be with the Lord forever."

We see then that the primary relationship in eternal life is between God and his people. Heaven could be most simply defined as "being with the Lord forever." In addition heaven will mean a continuing and unbreakable relationship with those we have loved on earth. We will be with them. Heaven is a *fellowship*, not a temple for private adoration.

Indeed, that is about all we can say about heaven with any certainty. The pictures to which I have already referred describe an existence that is sin- and pain-free, a realm where all our relationships are fulfilling and untarnished by the kind of faults that mar our lives on earth, and where everyone is content. But, above all, heaven is God-centered. All the images of it focus on God, or Jesus, as the hub or center. From his throne flows the life-giving river. If we do not want anything to do with God now, then it is unlikely that we will find his constant and conspicuous presence a source of contentment in the life beyond death. That is why the best preparation for heaven is not to read books about paradise, but to practice the presence of God here on earth. Those who know him in this life will feel immediately at home in heaven.

This is not to say that human relationships—transformed by the resurrection—will be unimportant in heaven. In one of the great Old Testament pictures of salvation, the story of Noah and the ark, it was not only the good man Noah who was saved from the flood, but also his wife, and their sons and daughters with their wives and husbands. The solidarity of the family is a principle that runs right through the Bible. St. Paul even argues that an unbelieving husband or wife is sanctified by a spouse's faith.[18] It is unlikely that this principle would be abandoned in heaven.

"God is love," St. John tells us. Our human loves are, at their best, reflections of God's love for us: "We love because he first loved us."[19] If anything at all survives death, surely it must be love. Faith and hope will be superseded by our own experience, but "love never fails." That is why "the greatest . . . is love."

In fact, as we have seen, our whole personality lives on in the resurrection, so it is unthinkable that the love which is its greatest attribute should not also live on, and indeed find its truest expression there. I believe that we shall not only recognize and be with our loved ones in heaven, but that we shall enjoy our relationship with them in a relaxed, contented, stress-free way that we could never experience on earth.

What about prayer for those who have died?

Questions about our relationships in heaven actually belong to the future. For the present, a more pressing question concerns our relationship with our dead loved ones now. As seen in the great creeds of the church, Christians affirm their belief in the "communion of saints," but it is probable that very few of them know what this means; or if they do, few put their belief into practice.

The communion of saints means the fellowship of believers—the unity of all those who are "in Christ." It speaks of the "communion," the sense of oneness, which embraces the minority of the church who are alive on the earth at any moment, and the great majority of the church who are already in the presence of God. Between those two groups lies death, like a narrow divide or a flimsy veil. All of us will one day cross that divide, discovering how insubstantial it really is. Until then, however, those of us on earth should not forget, or worse, ignore our fellow Christians already on the other side.

In the Catholic tradition, the dead are far from forgotten. They are prayed for at every mass, and often in private prayers. At the same time, the Virgin Mary and the "saints" are constantly approached with the words "pray for us," and are seen as persons interested in our affairs and active in intercession for the Christians on earth. All this makes the divide between earth and heaven seem less wide. Sometimes one feels it is almost transparent or nonexistent.

This tradition however, has taken serious abuse at various times in church history. The indulgences of the Middle Ages, tied in with the doctrine of purgatory (the notion of a place where the sins of baptized people are purged over a period of time before they are allowed to enter heaven) and the resulting belief that the living must help the dead through prayer, became a source of superstition and even financial exploitation.

Christians in the reformed traditions are still suspicious of the doctrine of purgatory, feeling that it perpetuates the idea of a second chance after death, and implies that the sacrifice of Jesus on the cross was not adequate to forgive *all* sins committed by anyone on earth. Evangelical Christians emphasize the completeness and sufficiency of this sacrifice, to which our prayers, good deeds, or acts of contrition add absolutely nothing. Consequently, they have rejected the idea of praying for the dead, claiming that such prayers cast doubt on the adequacy of what Jesus has done. If he has died for our sins—all of them, "the sin of the world"—how many sins remain to be dealt with in purgatory? If those who are dead and have trust in Jesus have eternal life—"he who has the Son has life"[20]—what more can we pray for them to receive in heaven?

We need to see, however, that the evangelical emphasis on the completeness of the gift of salvation sometimes has led Christians to a dangerous arrogance or presumption. We have talked as if all that matters is a single act of faith in Jesus and that thereafter there is no danger of relapse or possibility of failure. In fact, the New Testament's promises concerning the eternal security of the believer depend upon his being, remaining, or abiding in Christ. We recognize this need in practice when we pray for each other to remain steadfast in the faith.

These elements of evangelical thinking have led many Christians to a strange and awkward silence when it comes to the believing dead. I think it would be fair to say that there are many churches where the dead are simply never mentioned once the funeral is over. God is thanked for their lives, and then, it seems, they are erased from corporate memory. Perhaps this is a reaction against the excessive attention given to the dead in other religious traditions; but whatever the reason, it is a negative, unhelpful, and potentially damaging attitude. It is also contrary to the practice of the early church, and a denial, or at least a devaluation, of the doctrine of the communion of saints.

The book of Hebrews gives a quite different and much more positive picture of the relationship of Christians on earth to those already in heaven. The writer depicts the

earthly church as surrounded by a cloud of heavenly wit-
nesses, like a crowd of spectators in a vast arena.[21] As we
live out our lives on earth, those who have gone before us
watch and, perhaps, pray.

I say "perhaps" because there is no clear instance in the
New Testament of prayer for those on earth being offered
by or requested of a Christian in heaven. On the other
hand, it is clear that prayer *is* offered in heaven, and we
know that Jesus himself carries on an unceasing ministry
of intercession for his people.[22] It would seem fitting, then,
that the church in heaven should in some way share in
that ministry of Jesus.

However, their prayer for us is less in question than our
prayer for them. It may seem pointless to pray for loved
ones who have died. The Christian dead are with Christ,
removed from all the sin, pain, suffering, and anxiety of
the world. Isn't it superfluous to pray for them? What good
thing can we request for them that they do not already
have? And wouldn't offering such a prayer imply that life
in the very presence of the Lord is less than perfect?

These objections are reasonable, and indeed unanswerable, if we consider only intercessory prayer—prayer in
which we ask God for things on behalf of other people.
But most prayer in the Bible is not that kind. Prayer at its
highest is not *asking* but *communion*—being in the presence
of God, learning his will, deepening our love for him, and
drawing into that experience of fellowship those we love
and long for. Prayer, too, is "asking" for what we know to
be the will of God, and therefore what must inevitably
come about. This is not so much asking for something to
happen as it is aligning ourselves with God, sharing in his
purposes.

Jesus himself taught us to pray:

Our Father who art in heaven,
Hallowed be thy name.
Thy kingdom come.
Thy will be done, on earth
As it is in heaven.

These first three petitions or requests are in fact in this category of prayer that aligns the petitioner with God. There is nothing in all the universe so certain as the knowledge that ultimately God's will must be done, and that his kingdom must come. Yet we ask for it. Our purpose is not to achieve the unlikely, but to cooperate positively in the inevitable.

When we consider the believing dead, we find a similar situation. It is absolutely certain that they are happy and content in a realm of light, joy, and peace. Our prayers can reflect that. In a sense, we can share in their contentment. It is true that our prayers cannot improve their lot, but our understanding can be deepened and our faith strengthened as we pray. We can cooperate in the inevitable.

This means, in practice, that we do not pray *for* the dead so much as we pray *with* or *about* them. We certainly shouldn't remove their names from our prayers, as though they have ceased to exist. They are more "alive" now than they have ever been. They do not *need* our prayers, but that does not mean they do not value them as a sign of our continuing love for them and our common faith. And we certainly may find the act of praying for them helpful and reassuring in our own lives.

But how should we pray? If we are not asking anything on their behalf, what is there left to say? The answer is found in that word *communion.* Just as praying, at its highest, is not so much a matter of asking for things as of deepening our relationship with God, praying for people is not only a matter of asking for things on their behalf, but also of deepening our spiritual relationship with them in Christ.

Our prayers will include, rather than exclude, our loved ones who have died. We will not request things for them which we know they already have in perfection: forgiveness, acceptance with God, peace, joy, light, rest. Rather, we will recall thankfully their lives on earth, and celebrate and reaffirm our love for them. It also seems to me perfectly appropriate that our prayers express our anticipation of meeting these friends and relatives again. In other words, praying about the dead in this way means thinking about our loved ones before God—they in his immediate presence, we in his presence through prayer—and simply enjoying being united in him.

I believe that most bereaved people who are Christians will be helped by praying in this way, and by doing it regularly, perhaps on the same day each week or at a worship service on Sundays. It may disturb or upset some people to do this, and if so they can confidently leave their loved ones in God's hand, and return to praying for them later when it ceases to be so painful. For most people, however, prayer of this kind is deeply reassuring.

It is unhealthy to become unbalanced in any area of one's thought life, including the area of prayer. Sometimes a personal problem or ambition crowds everything else out of our prayers, and sometimes a person does, whether he is living or dead.

For a bereaved person there is obviously a danger that every time he turns to prayer, his thoughts—released from the business of daily life—will focus on that missing loved one. It is then all too easy for prayer to cease being God-centered and to become obsessed with the loved one who has died, and with one's own problems of loneliness or despair. When that happens, prayer, which should help to release us from our anxieties as we bring them before God, can actually increase them.

The most obvious answer would be to stop praying, or else to bar all reference in our prayers to the person who has died. Preferably, we should turn our obsession into a suitable prayer, and then discipline ourselves as to the amount of time we give the topic and how often we return to it. In other words, rather than ignore it, we can make the problem a matter of brief and deliberate prayer. And then we can turn, equally deliberately, to all those other elements in prayer which our obsession was in danger of rejecting. To do this, it may be necessary to pray more briefly than usual or in a different place or atmosphere, but it should not be necessary to abandon prayer altogether. (Some suitable prayers for or about our dead loved ones are given in an appendix at the end of this book, and they might also serve as a pattern for extemporaneous prayer.)

Can we ever make contact with those who have died?
Many bereaved people, in the months following a loved one's death, feel an almost irresistible urge to get into contact with them. At that moment the appeal of "spiritualism," which claims the possibility of that contact, may be very strong. A friend who is a spiritualist may suggest a visit to a seance, or the idea may come from reading something in a book or a magazine. It may seem harmless enough just to go along to a meeting, especially if it is described as a "Christian Spiritualist Church." Many of those who attend are undoubtedly sincere and sympathetic people. For the Christian, however, the practice is absolutely forbidden in the Bible and by the church; and

for anybody it is, I believe, a short-sighted, unhelpful, and even dangerous pursuit.

The central figure of any seance is the medium, through whom the spirits of the dead can speak to the living. The medium will deliberately open himself or herself to the spirit world, and very often messages will come through, voiced by the medium. These messages, purported to be the words and even the voices of the dead, are generally "proved" genuine by their mention of places and events known only to the spirit and the person to whom the message is directed. I remember one woman being very excited that her husband had come through from the "other side" to tell her to transfer some money into the Abbey National Building Society!

This brief and rather superficial "contact" with the dead at a seance is, of itself, completely unsatisfying. What often happens is that the living relative becomes more and more obsessed with the weekly sessions, clinging to this shadow of the loved one but failing to come to terms with the reality of death or, for that matter, resurrection. It is true that spiritualism reinforces a belief in a life beyond death, but not the full life—eternal life—of which the Bible speaks. Seances offer little more than a voice from the shadows, a pale substitute for the real thing. There is little evidence that spiritualism helps anybody to cope with bereavement or to resume a normal life afterwards. There is plenty of evidence that it can prevent a healthy recovery and lead to obsessive clinging to seances and "messages" instead of positive belief in the bodily resurrection of the loved one and eternal life with God in heaven.

However, even if one is tempted to seek some consolation in the practice of spiritualism, the temptation should be resisted because it is quite explicitly forbidden by God.

Spiritism, the attempt to establish contact with the dead through mediums, is as old as history. It is frequently mentioned—always disparagingly—in the Old Testament, and there are several clear warnings against it: "When men tell you to consult mediums and spiritists, who whisper and mutter, should not a people inquire of their God? Why consult the dead on behalf of the living?"[23]

This warning, in the words of the prophet Isaiah, is not simply a negative one. It points out the immense privilege we have because God exists as the focus of our prayers and requests for guidance. He knows all about our dead loved ones, as well as about our own needs and anxieties. Let us ask him about those we have lost, and let us listen to what his Word has to say to us about their security, their joy, and their peace in his presence. But let us not disturb ourselves (and even, perhaps, the dead) by using means of contact with the unseen world which God has forbidden. He is the Lord of all worlds, visible and invisible. He knows, as we do not, the dangers that lurk in the darker corners of the spirit world. It would be folly indeed to exchange the pure and joyful fellowship which all God's people can enjoy in the communion of saints for the dangerous and forbidden world of whispering spirits.

6

CHRISTIAN HOPE

Hope is one of the great words of Christianity, along with faith and love. This is not the weak, unsubstantiated optimism that we express when we say "I hope so," but a confident belief that what God has promised, he will do. Hope is at the heart of that positive, serene approach to life which has always marked Christian faith at its best.

And hope is the chief ingredient of a Christian's approach to bereavement. When all is said and done, when the tears have been shed and the loneliness and emptiness have been faced, the believer returns to this bedrock—hope.

No eye has seen,
no ear has heard,
no mind has conceived
what God has prepared for those who love him.[1]

So wrote St. Paul to the church at Corinth. Jesus' words express the same hope even more forcefully:

Do not let your hearts be troubled. Trust in God; trust also in me. In my Father's house are many rooms; if it

were not so, I would have told you. I am going there
to prepare a place for you. And if I go and prepare a
place for you, I will come back and take you to be with
me that you also may be where I am.[2]

The Christian hope is not simply that there is some kind
of life beyond death. It is that life in its fullness, life with
God, begins beyond the grave. Victor Hugo wrote:

When I go down to the grave, I can say like so many
others that I have finished my day's work; but I cannot
say that I have finished my life. Another day's work will
begin the next morning. The tomb is not a blind alley—it
is a thoroughfare. It closes with the twilight to open
with the dawn.

The hope is that God will keep his promises, will overcome
evil in the world and in us, and will bring his people into
his presence to live with him forever. Our destiny is not
to turn to dust on the surface of this lonely planet, but to
"glorify God and enjoy him forever," as the Westminster
Catechism puts it.

So heaven is not a strange place, but our home. That
was how St. Paul saw it: "We would prefer to be away
from the body and at home with the Lord."[3] Home is the
place of familiarity, where people speak our dialect, know
our ways, accept us without question. Home is where we
belong, the place of the family. It is the place we return to
at the end of a journey, drawn by familiar faces and voices.
Heaven is that kind of place.

When circumstances seem desperate or evil seems to
overpower us, it is this ultimate hope that guards our
hearts. Certainly in the most difficult days of bereavement,
during the lonely hours before dawn or the moments when
our loss stabs the mind without warning, it is to this hope
that we can cling. We are not engaged in mere wishful

thinking or blind optimism, but in commitment to one of the foundations of the Christian faith.

Christianity is a resurrection faith. It is about the victory God won over death when he raised Jesus. The Christian religion is not primarily a religion of law, or struggle, or dogma—though certainly all these things enter in. It is at its core a religion of new life. Jesus said that he had come "that they may have life, and have it to the full."[4] And St. John, writing at the end of the apostolic period, summed up in these words the testimony for which all the other apostles had given their lives: "This is the testimony: God has given us eternal life, and this life is in his Son."[5] In the opening sentences of the book of John, he said much the same thing: "In him [Jesus] was life, and that life was the light of men."[6]

So even in the darkest moments the Christian can have hope. There may be times when we don't feel hopeful, but the hope exists, because God exists. He raised Jesus, and has promised to raise all those who trust in Jesus. "We have this hope as an anchor for the soul, firm and secure."[7]

This is the counter to fear and self-pity. Faced by the reality of death, we may be more susceptible to a fear of death itself, either our own or that of those we love. But death is an enemy that has been conquered; Jesus has liberated us from this fear that has haunted humankind throughout history. As the writer of the letter to the Hebrews put it, Jesus shared in our humanity "so that by death he might destroy him who holds the power of death—that is, the devil—and free those who all their lives were held in slavery by their fear of death."[8]

Self-pity arises when we allow sorrow and deprivation to cloud our judgment, causing us to lose our vision of the eternal and see things in only temporal terms. "Our present sufferings," said Paul, "are not worth comparing with the glory that will be revealed in us."[9] We must grieve for our loved ones who are taken from us. We need feel no guilt about that. But self-pity is a different matter altogether. As Elisabeth Elliot has written, "I know of nothing more paralyzing, more deadly, than self-pity. It is death that has no resurrection, a sinkhole from which no rescuing hand can drag you because you have chosen to sink."

In the first days and weeks of our loss, as the brain adjusts and we slowly come to terms with our changed circumstances, hope may seem distant. Grief, even self-pity, may temporarily overpower us. But hope grounded in God cannot remain submerged. It will surface one day, probably sooner than we expect. And then we shall know, as we have never known before our bereavement, what Easter is all about. We will learn to live with our loss to the end of our days on earth. But we will also learn to live in hope—the hope of the resurrection, the hope of heaven.

We will not grieve without hope, but look forward to the eternal life God has promised us, when we will live with all those we have loved, and lost for a short while. This is a prospect every Christian can believe in and anticipate with joy. But those of us who have been through the valley of the shadow of death, who have known the loneliness and emptiness of mourning and have come through it to a new understanding of the Christian hope—we will savor that prospect with a joy others can seldom understand.

PRAYERS IN BEREAVEMENT

At the time of bereavement

Lord,
at this moment I am not aware of you.
All I can feel is the numb shock,
The emptiness,
The absence of someone deeply loved.
Help me through these next hours and days
To trust you in the darkness as I have
trusted you in the light.
For Jesus' sake. Amen.

Before a funeral

Heavenly Father,
Prepare and strengthen me for this occasion;
Not so that I do not grieve
But so that I do not lose hope.
Help me to say goodbye,
To let this loved one go,
'In sure and certain hope of the resurrection.'
May the faith of my friends and the
Faith of the church
Sustain me while my own faith cannot,
And may gratitude for the life that is ended
Unite me with all the others who will sorrow at its passing.
Lord, I believe.
Help me where faith falls short.
Lord, I trust you.
May I rest in your trustworthiness.
For Jesus' sake. Amen.

Father in heaven, you gave your son, Jesus Christ, to suffering and to death on the cross, and raised him to life in glory. Grant us a patient faith in time of darkness, and strengthen our hearts with the knowledge of your love; through Jesus Christ our Lord. Amen. *(from the Alternative Service)*

A prayer about the loved one

Lord of life, and Conqueror of death,
I thank you that (name) lives now in your presence,
Where there is no sorrow, pain, anxiety, or death.
Give him/her my love, and strengthen my sense of the unity
    that binds all your people together, in heaven and
    on earth.
Help me to have a constant faith in you, and so to live now
    with the knowledge that in your own good time I may
    enter your heaven of light and be reunited with (name)
    and all your people.
For Jesus' sake. Amen.

A prayer about the believing dead

Heavenly Father
We give you thanks and praise
For all those we have loved on earth
But see no longer.
As they rejoice in the realms of light
May we who are left
Follow their examples,
Enjoy their fellowship,
And look forward to that time when we and they will
    stand together before your throne and praise you.
    Through Jesus Christ our Lord. Amen.

A prayer for those who are bereaved

God our Father,
We pray for our friend who has been bereaved.
In this time of darkness, give him your light,
In this time of loneliness, your presence,
In this time of testing, your strength.
May we who love him share his sorrow,
Weeping with the weeper,
And may we give him time and understanding,
Until, in your good time, the wound is healed and the
    darkness is past.
For Jesus Christ's sake. Amen.

Some readings for a time of bereavement

Do not let your hearts be troubled. Trust in God; trust also
in me. In my Father's house are many rooms; if it were not
so, I would have told you. I am going there to prepare a
place for you. And if I go and prepare a place for you, I
will come back and take you to be with me that you also
may be where I am. (Jesus, in John 14:1-3, NIV)

I am the resurrection and the life. He who believes in me
will live, even though he dies; and whoever lives and believes in me will never die. (Jesus, in John 11:25–26, NIV)

In the account of the bush, even Moses showed that the
dead rise, for he calls the Lord "the God of Abraham, and
the God of Isaac, and the God of Jacob." He is not the
God of the dead, but of the living, for to him all are alive.
(Jesus, in Luke 20:37–38, NIV)

Christ has indeed been raised from the dead, the firstfruits of those who have fallen asleep. For since death came through a man, the resurrection of the dead comes also through a man. For as in Adam all die, so in Christ all will be made alive . . . Listen, I tell you a mystery: We will not all sleep, but we will all be changed—in a flash, in the twinkling of an eye, at the last trumpet. For the trumpet will sound, the dead will be raised imperishable, and we will be changed. For the perishable must clothe itself with the imperishable, and the mortal with immortality. When the perishable has been clothed with the imperishable, and the mortal with immortality, then the saying that is written will come true: "Death has been swallowed up in victory."

"Where, O death, is your victory?
Where, O death, is your sting?"

The sting of death is sin, and the power of sin is the law. But thanks be to God! He gives us the victory through our Lord Jesus Christ. (St. Paul, in 1 Cor. 15:20–22; 51–57, NIV)

Brothers, we do not want you to be ignorant about those who fall asleep, or to grieve like the rest of men, who have no hope. We believe that Jesus died and rose again and so we believe that God will bring with Jesus those who have fallen asleep in him. According to the Lord's own word, we tell you that we who are still alive, who are left till the coming of the Lord, will certainly not precede those who have fallen asleep. For the Lord himself will come down from heaven, with a loud command, with the voice of the archangel and with the trumpet call of God, and the dead in Christ will rise first. After that, we who are still alive and are left will be caught up with them in the clouds to meet the Lord in the air. And so we will be with the Lord

forever. Therefore encourage each other with these words.
(St. Paul, in 1 Thess. 4:13–18, NIV)

Then I saw a new heaven and a new earth, for the first
heaven and the first earth had passed away, and there was
no longer any sea. I saw the Holy City, the new Jerusalem,
coming down out of heaven from God, prepared as a bride
beautifully dressed for her husband. And I heard a loud
voice from the throne saying, "Now the dwelling of God
is with men, and he will live with them. They will be his
people, and God himself will be with them and be their
God. He will wipe every tear from their eyes. There will
be no more death or mourning or crying or pain, for the
old order of things has passed away." (The vision of John
on Patmos, Rev. 21:1–4, NIV)

We should thank God not only for the resurrection but
also for the *hope* of it. It is that hope which comforts us in
the face of bereavement and helps us to think of those
who have died with courage, and even joy. We know they
will rise again, and that we should meet them.

If we must sorrow, don't let us waste our sorrow on *them!*
Let's sorrow for those who live in sin, not for those who
die in faith. The apostle Paul once spoke of those for whom
he mourned—not those who had died, but those who are
alive and had not repented of their sins. Of course, we
shall—and we should—weep a little for those who have
left us, even though we know we shall see them again.
But we should weep far more for the folly of the sinner.

So let us be selective in our mourning. Let us get our
priorities in order. We should mourn for our sin, but for
nothing else that comes to us—not poverty, nor sickness,
nor injustice, nor abuse, nor untimely death. Whatever

human trial comes our way, let us bear it without resentment. We may well find that these calamities add not to our tears, but to our crowns. (John Chrysostom [A.D. 247–407] from *Faith under Fire)*

When a dear one dies, the unbeliever sees a corpse, but the Christian sees a body asleep. The unbeliever says that the dead person has "gone." We agree, but we remember *where* he has gone. He has gone where the apostle Paul is, where Peter is, where the whole company of the saints is. We remember that he will rise, not with tears of dismay, but with splendor and glory. (John Chrysostom from *Faith under Fire)*

It's a wonderful thought that at this moment friends of ours, people we have known and loved, are at the side of the Lord in heaven, sharing his joy as once they shared his pains. Their hearts were never wedded to this world and its values, but were focused on him who died for us, and was raised from the dead for us by God.

So copy them, as they copied Christ. (Polycarp of Smyrna [A.D. 69–155] from *Faith under Fire)*

Death, be not proud, though some have called thee
Mighty and dreadful, for thou art not so:
For those whom thou think'st thou dost overthrow
Die not, poor Death; nor yet canst thou kill me.
From rest and sleep, which but thy picture be,
Much pleasure, then from thee much more must flow;
And soonest our best men with thee do go—
Rest of their bones and souls' delivery!
Thou'rt slave to fate, chance, kings, and desperate men,
And dost with poison, war, and sickness dwell;

And poppy or charms can make us sleep as well
And better than thy stroke. Why swell'st thou then?
One short sleep past, we wake eternally,
And Death shall be no more: Death, thou shalt die!
(John Donne [1573–1631])

NOTES

Chapter 1/The Shocking Event
1   Christopher Leach,
    Letter to a Younger Son,
    Arrow Books

Chapter 2/Not the End
1   David Winter, *Here-
    after*, Harold Shaw
    Publishers
2   Eccles. 12:7
3   1 Cor. 15:53
4   Acts 2:24, 31–32
5   1 Cor. 15:54

Chapter 3/The Healing Funeral
1   Acts 20:38
2   Trevor Lloyd, *Ministry
    and Death*, Grove Book-
    lets

*Chapter 4/Getting Back
to Normal*
1   Derek Nuttall, "Be-
    reavement and After,"
    New Society, 14 January
    1982

*Chapter 5/Questions People
Ask*
1   I have tried to set out
    this evidence in my
    book *The Search for the
    Real Jesus*, Hodder &
    Stoughton
2   1 Cor. 15
3   John 3:16
4   1 Cor. 15
5   John 10:10 (NEB)
6   2 Cor. 5:21

7   Rev. 20:11ff
8   Cf 1 Cor. 15;
    1 Cor. 3:11–15;
    Rom. 2:12–16
9   Heb. 9:27
10 Rom. 2:14–15
11 Rom. 3:23
12 Rom. 2:14–16
13 2 Pet. 3:9
14 Rev. 7:9
15 Rev. 21:4–5
16 Rev. 22:1–3
17 Cf 1 Thess. 4:13–18
18 1 Cor. 7:14
19 1 John 4:19
20 1 John 5:12

21 Heb. 12:1
22 Heb. 7:25
23 Isa. 8:19

Chapter 6/Christian Hope
1   1 Cor. 2:9
2   John 14:1–3
3   2 Cor. 5:8
4   John 10:10
5   1 John 5:11
6   John 1:4
7   Heb. 6:19
8   Heb. 2:14–15
9   Rom. 8:18